MR PEEK'S POETRY FUNTIME

BOOK TWO
SOME OLD, SOME NEW

(21 more poems for a classroom full of fun)

By

Tony Peek

BOOK

I opened up a picture book
And disappeared inside,
A world filled up with fun and games
Where I could stay and hide.

I laughed at silly creatures
I giggled at funny words,
I let myself be carried away
By the songs of singing birds.

I read the book till way past late
Then I turned out my light,
To sleep and dream of all I'd seen
In my picture book that night.

LITTLE WORDS

The little words are biggest
The little words are best,
The words like 'Please' and 'Thank you'
Are much better than the rest.

I love the way the little words
Make other people smile,
Like when I say 'I love you'
Or 'I'll be back in a while'.

It makes me happy I can use
Every thought and every letter,
To try and make this world of ours
A little bit more better.

SALLY SUE

Sally Sue the butcher's dog
She loved all kinds of meat,
Pork and veal and venison
They all went down a treat.

But sausages, sausages, sausages
Were the thing she loved the best,
She dined upon them night and day
And never stopped to rest.

But then one day the butcher
Not meaning to be rude,
Mistook his dog for sausages
And she became her food!

BETTER WORLD

Can we not make a world
Where everything is good?
Can we not make a world
Where things work as they should?

Can we not make a better place
For everyone to live?
Can we not make a better place
Where all are pleased to give?

Of course we can, of course we can
And that's what we will do,
We'll make a world that's good for all
And not just for the few.

DOCTOR, DOCTOR

Doctor, doctor help me quick
You see I'm feeling really sick,
I used to be quite big and tall
But now I'm shrunk and really small.

I've got fur where I once had skin
And grown a tail that's long and thin,
I've got small whiskers and small feet
And all I want is cheese to eat.

I move my mouth but I can't speak
All I do is squeak, squeak, squeak,
I'd love to scamper round your house
I think I've turned into a mouse.

FOOTBALLER

I want to be a footballer
So I'm practicing my skills,
I'm doing lots of fitness stuff
And loads and loads of drills.

I'm practicing with both feet
Because one is not enough,
Being a pro footballer
Is really, really tough.

I know that I can do it though
And dad's going to help me out,
He's always on the sidelines
Trying not to shout.

I want to be a footballer
And that's what I'm going to be,
I'm not a silly day dreamer
Just you wait and see.

I'm going to play for Manchester
Or Chelsea or Madrid,
And one day all the world will talk
About the things I did.

Yes, I'm going to be a footballer
I'll have money and have fame,
And everywhere I go and play
The crowd will cheer my name.

SAD TOMATO

I am sad tomato
I'm the last one on the plant,
You see I'm left here hanging
Where all the others aren't.

I am a sad tomato
I'm lonely as can be,
There's no one here upon the vine
Except poor lonesome me.

I should be in a salad
Or on some bread with cheese,
Or in a bowl of pasta
Or in a tube to squeeze.

I should be feeling biting teeth
Or be in a bowl of soup,
I shouldn't be here all alone
With these sad old leaves that droop.

I am a sad tomato
But I'm sure I will taste good,
If you could come and chop me up
And eat me like you should.

RUSSIAN DOLL

I am a Russian doll
There are lots of bits of me,
But I can hide inside myself
As you yourself can see.

I'm very, very big
But I'm also very small,
I'm teeny, teeny, tiny
But I'm also really tall.

I am a Russian doll
I'm smiley and I'm kind,
Open up my body
And see how many mes you find.

KINDER EGG SURPRISE

My mummy bought me a Kinder egg
And I can't wait to see,
What there is inside it
And what prize there is for me.

I hope it's a little princess
Or a speedy racing car,
I got a little monkey once
Swinging from a bar.

I got a Barbie, got a bike
I got a unicorn,
I got a little puppy
That had only just been born.

So now we're home, we're home at last
And I start to whine and beg,
But mum says only after lunch
Can I have my Kinder egg.

So, of course, I eat up everything
Then she brings me a little plate,
And the Kinder egg is on it
And I can hardly wait.

I slowly peel the coloured foil
And I smell the tasty treat,
And I feel the yummy chocolate
Which I crack open and eat.

The brown and white I love it
And hidden underneath,
Is the little plastic, oval ball
Which I open with my teeth.

Then I hold it out in both my hands
And it's there before my eyes,
My brand-new, fun-filled tiny toy
My Kinder egg surprise.

SQUARE

They say I am a rectangle
But I don’t really care,
All my sides are equal
So I know I’m a square.

SHINE A LIGHT

Shine a light, shine a light
Into the darkest of places,
Shine a light, shine a light
Into the saddest of faces.

Let tomorrows all be better
Let's forget sad yesterdays,
Let the light of love shine on us all
And help us mend our ways.

Let the world be full of wonder
Let the world be full of joy,
Let there be a smiling happy face
On every girl and boy.

THE SOUNDS I LOVE

The sounds I love, the sounds I love
I love them all you know,
I love to hear the rain
Or hear the silence of the snow.
I love to hear a happy laugh
I love when music's loud,
I love to hear the roar and cheer
Of a happy football crowd.

The sounds I love, the sounds I love
Around me every day,
The noise of pouring water
Or the leaves I kick away.
The sounds of drummers drumming
Or Lego in a box,
Or late at night, when I'm awake
The barking of a fox.

The sounds I love, the sounds I love
Don't you just love them too?
And which of all the sounds we have
Are the ones loved most by you?

THE BADGER & UNICORN

The badger and the unicorn
The leopard and the snake,
Gathered on a tiny beach
Beside a great big lake.

They played a game of billiards
They played a game of pool,
They played a game of something else
Because it sounded cool.

The snake said she was hungry
The leopard chased a bird,
The badger told the unicorn
Its horn was quite absurd.

The party ended sadly
When the leopard ate the snake,
And the badger bit the unicorn
Who kicked him in the lake.

SPRING FLOWERS

Little flower bulbs
Down in the dark,
Lying so silently
Suddenly spark.

The weather is warmer
They're longing to grow,
After months in the ground
Beneath rain, frost and snow.

They start to expand
They spread out their roots,
They gradually grow
They push up small shoots.

And up in the fields
In the woods and the park,
We see their green tips
Appear out of the dark.

The Crocus, the Daffodil
The Tulips all rise,
With the Hyacinth and Iris
They stretch to the skies.

And we people above
In the lovely Spring air,
We stand in amazement
And in wonder we stare.

At the beauty around us
As nature's unfurled,
And we think to ourselves
What a wonderful world.

HOMEWORK

I never do no homework
I'm much too smart you see,
I don't need no extra stuff
It's too easy for me.

No, I never do my homework
I do as I please,
You don't need no maths or sciences
To work in Mackey Dees.

I don't do my homework
And I'm much smarter than you,
No, I don't do my homework
I've got betterer things to do.

PUPPY DOGS

I love all little puppy dogs
They are so cute and fun
I love to watch them waddling
I love to watch them run.

I love the way they bounce around
I love to hear them bark,
I love to see them see themselves
In the windows after dark.

I love all little puppy dogs
I love the way they eat,
I love to see them rushing round
On their tiny tumbling feet.

I'd love to get a puppy dog,
I think that would be great,
But mum says our house is too small
And a dog will have to wait.

EATING FLOWERS

I'm sitting in the garden
Eating lots of flowers,
I can sit and eat them all
For hours and hours and hours.

And when I'm feeling really full
I rush up to the loo,
And have a little wee-wee
And do a great big poo.

I LOVE BUTTER

I love butter
And I don't think it makes me fat,
I love butter
What do you think about that?

I love butter
On bits of bread and toast,
I love butter
It's the thing I love the most.

I love butter
And the more the better too,
I love butter
Margarine's just stinky goo.

STRING

I had a little piece of string
I tied it to my toes,
But then it started growing
Until it reached my nose.

All at once I realized
It wasn't string at all,
But a great big sliding, slithering snake
That measured six feet tall.

I gave the snake a place to sleep
A pillow and a bed,
I gave him mice to gobble up
And chose to call him Fred.

A CUP OF TEA

I like to drink a cup of tea,
When it's time to go to bed,
It's nice and warm and comforting
And relaxes my head.

I boil the kettle and get a cup
And I put a teabag in,
Then I get a little biscuit
That's nice and fresh and thin.

And when the tea is ready
I dip the biscuit for a while,
And then I eat it quickly
And it always makes me smile.

IN JUST A LITTLE WHILE

It's time for me to leave you now
It's time to say goodbye,
I've had such a lot of fun
I almost want to cry.

It's time for me to leave you now
Though I don't want to go,
But thanks so much for having me
It's been great fun you know.

So thanks for having me today
I hope I've made it clear,
That I would love to come again
Perhaps this time next year?

So even though it's time to go
I'll sing a little tune,
For I'll be coming back to see you
Very, very soon.

Although it's time for me to leave
I'll be back in just a while,
So don't feel bad, and don't feel sad
Just wave and give a smile.

I hope you have enjoyed:
Book Two Some old, some new

Book One:
Some Old Some New: 21 Rhyming Poems
Is available on Amazon

There are three other books available from my website

Bits & Bobs: (Mr Peek's Poetry Funtime Volume 1)
Nice & New: (Mr Peek's Poetry Funtime Volume 2)
After Dark (Mr Peek's Poetry Noire Volume 1)

www.mrpeekpoetry.co.uk

www.ingramcontent.com/pod-product-compliance
Ingram Content Group UK Ltd.
Pitfield, Milton Keynes, MK11 3LW, UK
UKHW042002190726
13854UKWH00005B/2122

9 789780 954116